RAINBOW MAGIC

For Elizabeth,
love, light &
Blessings,
Chrissy Greenslade
x

Rainbow Magic

Book Four

Poetry by Chrissy Greenslade.
Illustrations by Jenny Williams.

PETRA PUBLISHING

RAINBOW MAGIC

Copyright © Chrissy Greenslade. 2002

ISBN: 0-9534319-3-2

First Edition published Summer 2002 by
PETRA PUBLISHING
4, Leven Close
Bournemouth
BH4 9LP

" I dedicate this book
to my dear sister Enid, my brothers,
Sidney and Donald and to all my 'sisters and brothers'
throughout the world. "

Also by Chrissy Greenslade:
Book One - Rainbow of Life
Book Two - Rainbow of The Heart
Book Three - Rainbow of Love

British Library Cataloguing in Publication Data:
A catalogue record for this book is available from the British Library

Printed in China through World Print Ltd.

Layout & Design Mark A Fudge
design@fudgie.co.uk / www.fudgie.co.uk

CONTENTS

ACKNOWLEDGEMENTS

The following poems of mine have previously been published in the following magazines and annuals.

Secrets

Christmas Eve
First Sight of The Sea
My Fisherman
Letter From A Friend

The Lady

Peace

My Weekly

My Contact With Lenses
The Collector

Wealth Beyond Riches
(Anthology)

Cleansing The Temple

This England

My Special Tree

The Journal (DHWSHA)

Make Up Your Mind
Acceptance

The Science of Thought Review
(Now 'New Vision')

Meditation

Grace Magazine

Peace

Chrissy Greenslade thanks all her readers,
who sent such wonderful letters.
If you wish to be informed of forthcoming books in
the Rainbow Series and Stockists please contact:

Petra Publishing,
4, Leven Close,
Bournemouth,
BH4 9LP

Telephone: 01202 762730

E-mail: chrissy@petrapublishing.co.uk   www.petrapublishing.co.uk

INTRODUCTION

For my large, loving family of readers who have been awaiting my fourth book, I bring you Book Four, 'Rainbow Magic'. I hope it will fill you with as much pleasure and comfort as my previous three books. You will find there are many poems in this book which have a special meaning for you.

Once again I have included a few excerpts from some of my readers who so kindly took the time to write and show their appreciation. I will include other excerpts in my next books. Your wonderful response to my books makes my busy life worthwhile.

I have been guided by God in many directions this past year and my Rainbow books are now being read in retirement homes, at meetings, churches, talks, wedding and christening ceremonies. They are also being enjoyed and used by young people for study and poetry projects.

As you know I am non-profit making. My life's work is to share with you my poems which come from the heart and which I hope will touch your heart. Again in my 'Rainbow Series,' I share with you my love, comfort, laughter, faith and joy, hoping that my poems will uplift you and enhance your every day life.

I am still aiming to reach the end of my rainbow and with your support, I know I shall succeed. I have already started the fifth of my seven books, 'Rainbow Promise.'

If you know an elderly lady called Eileen, (I don't know her surname), whom I met at my Petra Publishing stand at a craft fair, please will you give her a message. Tell her that I have written the poem that I promised her, when she told me about the rainbow she saw when her husband was ill. 'A Rainbow for Eileen' is on Page 50.

You and I can face the future with courage. All things are possible. 'Expect a Miracle'. Once again take my hand my friend and cross over the rainbow with me.

Love and Light, Chrissy

For further information, book requirements, poetry readings and talks please contact
Chrissy Greenslade, Petra Publishing, 4 Leven Close, Bournemouth BH4 9LP
Tel: 01202 762730   E-mail address: chrissy@petrapublishing.co.uk
Internet website address: http://www.petrapublishing.co.uk

CHRISTMAS EVE

Last minute shoppers throng the streets,
Their bags and trolleys bulging,
Excited children tug and plead,
Their eager hopes divulging.

Bright, fairy lights and Christmas trees,
In shop windows are glowing,
And tiny tots with shining eyes,
Call out because it's snowing.

Behind each curtain families
Relax and wait with joy,
To celebrate the birthday
Of the holy, baby boy.

Around the earth, snow-blanketed,
Peace steals and smooths out stress,
Whilst Christmas magic casts its spell,
Of hope and happiness.

Bewitched by loving feelings
And by unity and love,
Snow feathers soft as angel wings,
Drift down from heaven above.

As carol-singers join the sounds
Of jollity and mirth,
The Christmas bells are ringing out
Their call for peace on earth.

I'VE COOKED MY GOOSE

Because I'm always writing there is not much time to cook,
So ready meals and microwaves help me get off the hook,
But sometimes I feel guilty that my meals are not home-made,
But as my time's so precious they're not often I'm afraid.

Today my dear old Auntie Kate said she would visit me,
And I've decided that there'll be something I've cooked for tea.
So I have made my mind up just for her I'll make a cake,
I have a scrumptious recipe of one I used to bake.

I search but cannot find it but I know it off by heart,
Enthusiasm is gripping me, I cannot wait to start.
I'll measure all ingredients, crack eggs, give now a stir,
Quite proud I can remember with no recipe to refer.

It really smells delicious, though it seems gooey and thick,
It's cooked now, but it just won't budge, to the tin it means to stick.
I'll have to scoop the cake out for the water I've forgotten
To add to it! So I decide - though I am feeling rotten -

That I will make some custard
 and pretend it is a sweet,
It tastes alright – well certainly
 – it's good enough to eat.
So now I'm calling gaily,
 "This fruit pudding I have made."
My blushing cheeks and
 downcast eyes, my secret now betrayed.

My Auntie's picked her spoon
 up but too late I give a shout,
For biting in my pudding
 she has pulled her false teeth out!

GOD'S HARVEST

There are harvests of fishes,
And harvests of corn,
There've been all kinds of harvests
Since mankind was born.

There are harvests of fruit,
Every food of its kind,
But the harvest of God
Is the one of the mind.

As we gather good thoughts,
We will cast out the bad,
As we store happy memories,
We'll forget all the sad.

As we gather our dreams,
We're filled then with hope,
When we gather God's strength.
With life's lessons we'll cope.

We won't store up our smiles,
We will give them away,
Echo words we've received,
In the nice things we say.

Let's collect all kind actions,
Put them into play,
Then what a wonderful harvest,
We'll celebrate today.

MY DAUGHTER'S DILEMMA

Her mind won't keep still,
She is feeling quite ill,
She will jump when the phone starts to ring;
She is moody and quick,
Sometimes sad, can feel sick,
She'll be full of contentment and sing.

She's full of despair,
Then she's up in the air,
She will race to the door for the post;
She takes ages to dress,
Says her hair is a mess,
And she lives on dry biscuits and toast.

She wants to look slim,
Cries at the slightest whim,
Is offended at the smallest thing;
She walks round in a dream,
And then she lets off steam,
With the joy that some flowers can bring.

I watch with concern,
But there's nothing to learn,
For her symptoms need my sympathy;
It's what we've all been through,
Just like me and like you,
For the cure is not simple you see.

But the moment I feel,
That this time it's for real,
Calm will spread on the wings of a dove;
That's the time I shall know
To let my daughter go,
Yes she's eighteen and madly in love!

MY BELOVED SISTER

How dearly I love you, my special, dear sister,
You're so kind and thoughtful to family and friends,
You're loving and caring, your whole life you're sharing,
Your tireless devotion and help never ends.

We live far apart yet in thought we're together,
We both want the best for the dear ones we love,
You put yourself last, always comforting, giving,
But you'll always cope with God's help from above.

As children we played, though we both were quite different,
For I was so noisy, the quiet one was you,
We went to the pictures, shared scrapbooks together,
We laughed and we cried, hoped our dreams would come true.

We both had our growing pains, marriages, anguish,
Our lessons in life brought us closer each day,
When older but stronger, together no longer,
We coped with whatever fate brought on life's way.

In our golden years now we go on believing,
We still are the young girls who're living inside,
Old age we're defying, for youth we're not crying,
We'll face what arrives and take it in our stride.

We'll learn to accept now our speeded up birthdays,
And welcome each day like a guiding new star,
Oh I am so glad I have such a nice sister,
And you'll find my love is wherever you are.

WE AGREE TO DIFFER

However much you love your partner,
Though you're faithful through
  and through,
Some ways you will find quite naturally
Very different from you.

If like me you feel the cold days,
Need three woollies if there's frost,
Being warm's essential living,
Heat full on and blow the cost.

When I'm cold, I'm edgy, tetchy,
When I'm warm, I'm mellow, glad,
But my loved one's roasting, toasting,
Much too hot and feeling bad.

Do you like to place the bedclothes,
Tucked around you neat and tight,
Or your man prefer it 'airy,'
With his feet poked out at night?

What about his tastes in eating?
Indian curries I have tried,
Loving him I want to please him,
Though the smell turns my inside.

Sometimes tastes in music differ,
As I play a loved refrain –
"What on earth is that she's singing?
Oh poor girl she is in pain!"

Are you quiet in the morning?
Do you like to stay in bed?
Or are you up bright and early,
Longing to get things ahead?

Do you like things neat and tidy?
Does he find this is a bind?
Do you love nick-knacks and clutter,
Or is he the Spartan kind?

Differences are a blessing,
Opposites are never bored,
When one's hasty, one is careful,
You'll find unity restored.

Little things can cause frustration,
But the test is fair and true,
Would you really like to live with,
Someone else who's just like you?

If always your life was perfect,
Things in place, always in tune,
You would find life lacked a challenge,
You'd soon tire of the honeymoon.

For our purpose is what matters,
And the care and love we show,
I wouldn't really change my loved one-
But why does he wear that dickey
  bow?

PICTURES IN THE SKY

I held my breath and gazed in awe,
Enthralled in pictures that I saw,
A castle turreted on high,
Its towers hidden in the sky.

A glistening lake, tranquil and still,
A fiery dragon on a hill,
White horses race, manes flying free,
A dream world seen but fleetingly.

I know this kingdom soon will go,
Be lost to mortals here below,
I hold my breath as they pass by,
My magic pictures in the sky.

SONIA'S CHRISTMAS WISH

Oh dear, how will he wrap it for Christmas,
The gift for which Sonia has asked?
It's big and it's round and it's hollow,
And it spins, where there's skill, very fast.

Now I know there's a problem to bring it,
For how will it go in his sack?
With all of the gifts he is carrying,
It's so awkward to fit on his back.

What a problem! But Santa will solve it,
It's what she's expecting from him,
I hope that he won't disappoint her,
For she wants to lose weight and be slim.

But I smile at the thought of our Sonia,
In nightdress, hair net and bare feet,
Attempting to spin as she wiggles,
But for John it will be such a treat.

For when inches are lost from her waistline,
She'll find there's no problem to stoop,
And as she will be feeling much fitter,
Don't forget Santa her Hoola Hoop!

ALONE IN IBIZA

A female on her own,
I was always alone,
No-one smiled but gave curious glances;
"If she wants to come here,
Without her 'Near and dear,'
On my husband she'll make some
advances.

If we speak she will cling,
Is she wearing a ring?
It's a lover I'm sure she is after,
Well, she's not getting mine,
Look, she's drinking red wine,
The head waiter's now filled her
with laughter!"

But what they didn't know,
Just a fortnight ago,
On arriving in Spain how I'd cried,
At the grave heart attack,
A nightmare looking back,
That first night when my man
nearly died.

But I knew I must cope,
Armed with toothpaste and soap,
My sole comrades of that dreadful night,
Whilst he fought for his breath,
My love close to his death,
How I prayed he'd not give up the fight.

So I walked all alone,
Now mature, fully grown,
As I wished that a smile came my way,
They weren't really to blame,
Some females played a game,
But time's flown,
This is my special day.

From now on they can stare,
Not alone but a pair,
For from hospital at last he is free,
Not a frown, I shall share,
No cold look, curious glare,
But a smile – for my husband's with me!

I COULD SAY A CROSS WORD!

I'm getting so excited,
For I have only three
More words to fill in then I might,
Have my first victory.

I'm not an intellectual,
I often claim defeat,
But trembling I feel that tonight,
My crossword I'll complete.

I haven't used the dictionary,
So far it has gone well,
I haven't asked for help with
General knowledge, how to spell.

Oh, I've just solved another,
Now there are only two,
And if they aren't too difficult,
Then my dreams will come true.

I've found one more solution,
My heart is beating fast,
If I can fill in thirteen down,
I'll have success at last.

What! I just don't believe it,
A name I've never heard!
So reluctantly I have to ask,
"Will you help me with this word?"

MAYTIME

The blackbird knows it's Maytime,
So does the bumblebee,
Azaleas and bluebells,
Are wonderful to see.

The mating game now settled,
Birds search for insect, seeds,
And flowers are bright and blooming,
As springtime warmth succeeds.

The young leaves light-green masses,
Paint gems of different hues,
And garden walls are splattered,
With alpines reds and blues.

Grass lush, refreshed with showers,
Competes with trees pale greens,
A blackbird in the birdbath,
Splashes, then shakes and preens.

The wind is spent and lazy,
As hazy skies remain,
I am so glad the sun has come
To bless Maytime again.

THE FLYING VISIT

His confidence was quite superb,
As he reversed the car,
An awkward, difficult approach,
Although not very far,
"I've done that really well, I think,"
My husband said to me,
"I need about another foot
As far as I can see."

"I'll have a look," I volunteered,
Opening the door a bit,
But when I saw how close we were,
I nearly had a fit.
"No, stop!" I yelled, but soon I knew,
That it was far too late,
The car wheels had gone down a step,
Into a garden gate.

Panic set in and frantic cries
Of "Help, what have I done?"
Came from inside the Volvo from
My distraught, wild-eyed one.
When whizzing tyres resisted and
The door completely jammed,
We finally decided it
Remained where it had rammed.

Just like a scalded kitten then
I rushed around, bright red,
When calm and cool and positive,
I should have been instead.
Our relatives returned back home,
To greet and welcome us,
They soon found out about the car,
The damaged gate, the fuss.

With calmness and efficiency,
They handled all with care,
And as their laughter drowned
  our fears,
I soon became aware,
That as I went to treat a cut,
With ointment and with plaster,
How funny and not terrible,
Had been our near disaster.

The damage wasn't very much.
More stress, worry and strain,
But we are really wondering,
Will they ask us there again?

- 20 -

ACCEPTANCE

It isn't always easy
To accept what each day brings,
Both the difficult and painful,
Or sad, frustrating things.

But if we pray about them,
Put each moment in God's hand,
Asking Him for strength and guidance,
He'll help us understand.

Our life is full of testings,
With His aid life fills with hope,
In accepting them with courage
And faith, we'll find we'll cope.

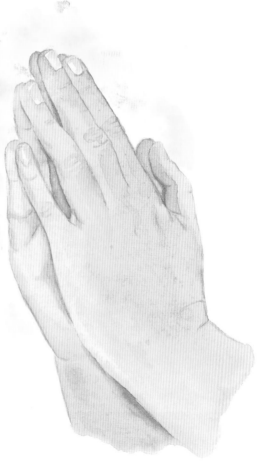

TIME FOR A CLEAR OUT

"Oh dear me," I said, as I gazed at the clutter,
"I must have a clear out!" I grumble and mutter.
I've too many ornaments, wardrobes are bulging,
Nick-nacks here and there where I'm over-indulging.

I don't want to keep them; I'm really not keen,
But friends will be hurt if their gifts are not seen.
Though some make me sigh, many others give pleasure,
Some are dust collectors but others I treasure.

I've kept empty boxes and jars and containers,
I've too many saucepans and basins and strainers,
Crammed tight are my book-shelves, I know they need thinning,
I've sorted out one shelf at least I'm beginning.

I've too many scarves, too much make-up and undies,
And blouses I wear only High Days and Sundays,
Far too many biscuits, tinned food in my coffers,
No more get one free, any more special offers.

So I'm on a spree to reduce what I'm keeping,
I feel overwhelmed and it's stopping me sleeping,
Tomorrow I'll sort out, get rid of more clothing,
But making decisions is what I am loathing.

For some might be useful or they're sentimental,
Are reasons I keep things, oh I'm going mental!
This style might come back, this huge vase is an heirloom,
I give up, I'll leave them for they still have house-room.

I'm feeling quite chilly, where is my red sweater?
I'm glad that I kept it, as I'm getting better.
I wish I could find it now it's time to stop,
Oh it's in the bag for the charity shop!

FIRST SIGHT OF THE SEA

The sea lay glistening as they gazed,
Mouths open totally amazed,
Their faces pressed against the pane,
Ignoring splattering spots of rain,
They called and called and called again,
"Oh, look the sea!"

The train it ran beside the sea,
Herring gulls cried," We're free, we're free!"
The children sniffed and smelt seaweed,
Chuckled at seagulls spite and greed.
They longed to splash, bare-foot, bare kneed,
In the sea.

And paddle they did, romped, laughed and played,
In sunlit waters unafraid,
Scampered with joy where sea birds wade,
Were proud of the castle and moat they made.
How they loved the beach, the house where they stayed,
By the sea.

Brisk rub of towel, sun-soft and dry,
The love of parents sat close by,
Beach picnics, cafes, terns on high,
Games and new friends – how time flew by!
Till sadly, "Goodbye," they said with a sigh,
And left the sea.

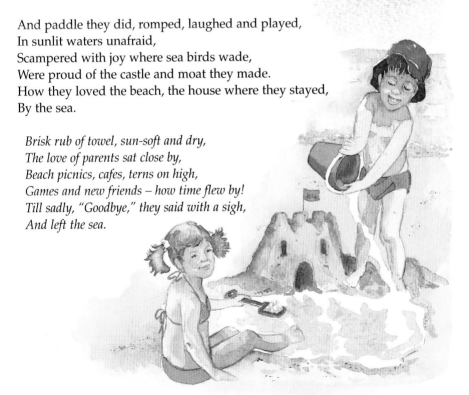

CHOCOHOLIC

I know that I shouldn't have,
I know that I wouldn't have,
Just done it at all
If it hadn't been there!

And I knew that I shouldn't do,
What next week I wouldn't do,
For Christmas is here,
Such temptation is rare.

I've just thrown the box away,
And thrown diet plans away,
I've eaten all the chocolates,
And I just don't care!

FEELINGS

Watching you suffer I felt my heart breaking,
As I felt helpless to remove your pain,
Then I felt hopeful as little by little,
Signs indicated you might live again.

Numbed were my feelings when you lost your battle,
Defeat reflected in your dear, kind eyes,
Suddenly I had to live here without you,
No time to hold you or say our goodbyes.

Sad were my feelings yet happy in knowing,
That you were whole and from pain you were free,
Bravely I coped as life stopped and restarted,
Knowing my darling that you were with me.

God gave me strength as I thought of your new life,
Happy and youthful, at peace, living on,
Of course I wept for myself as I missed you,
My dearest friend, my beloved had gone.

My faith restored me, I knew without question,
Short is the time you'll be out of my sight,
As problems faced me and I made decisions,
You would be helping me to get things right.

Now I've accepted and I'll be directed,
You'll help me know in bad times what to do,
Wonderful was the life we spent together,
How glad I am my love, God sent me you.

MY CONTACT WITH LENSES

It began when I was fifteen and I couldn't see the board,
They gave me pink-framed glasses that I hated and abhorred,
I wouldn't wear them till I must then thrust them on my face,
So bright red and self-conscious my replies were a disgrace.
This made the whole class titter, stare and smile and laugh at me,
I'd snatch the hideous glasses off as miserable as could be.

I then worked in a library and found just as before,
To read the titles on top shelves, the hateful things I wore.
"Oh dear, what a great pity," they all cried, "at seventeen!"
Their comments caused me agony, where confidence had been.
"Your blue eyes look so charming. Please don't hide them out of sight."
I took them off but made my world confused, less clear and bright.

Then one fine day I took the plunge and saw a new optician,
He gave me contact lenses; I achieved my life's ambition.
I walked around, my head held high, content with what I saw,
I rushed and bought a wide-brimmed hat, I wouldn't wear before.
Now without frames, my confidence and life was clear and new,
For with my contact lenses all my visions had come true!

CLEANSING THE TEMPLE

Our body is a temple,
To maintain pure and whole,
It needs to be kept holy now
To purify our soul.

For everything that enters,
Must be controlled and good,
So that our body can behave
Exactly as it should.

It doesn't need excesses.
It mustn't be abused,
For it is God's intention,
Our body should be used

To serve mankind, to love Him,
That is what life is for,
To live our life progressing,
As we live for evermore.

Our body is a temple,
In which our spirits dwell,
We'll make it whole and healthy,
For good thoughts will make it well.

As Jesus cleansed the temple,
So we can do the same,
To make our body a fitting place,
To hold the Holy Flame.

I'M NOT REALLY FORGETFUL

"What did I come in here for?" Oh I'm sure you say it too,
For these forgetful moments will come right out of the blue.
I'm really not forgetful, but where is my shopping list?
I must write down these items so that nothing will be missed.

So often when I've settled with my crossword, cup of tea,
I cannot find the glasses that I'll need to watch T.V.
I'm not really forgetful, well at least that's what I say,
Yet if I'm given directions I will still go the wrong way.

I need to ask the name again of someone I have met,
The face is quite familiar but her first name I forget.
I'm very good with birthdays for each month I take a look,
And write it on my memo - Oh, where is my birthday book?

However I'm not dwelling on the things I have forgotten,
Or I will really get depressed, feel old, and that is rotten.
So what I have remembered are the things I'll think about,
Like locking doors, making phone calls, putting milk bottles out.

I've posted letters, paid my bills –the postman's on his way,
It's not the postman, I forgot! Oh this has made my day!
Where did I leave my duster? Help! I mustn't make a fuss,
Because my hair's in rollers and the vicar's visiting us!

PEACE

Peace creeps up unexpectedly,
And takes me by surprise,
It comes upon me unawares,
Like sunshine in the skies.

A flower's scent or lovely hue,
Arouses all my senses,
A raucous rook, a pigeon pair,
Break down my last defences.

A celandine with golden petals,
Waiting to be counted,
A quiet lane all clothed in may,
A stile which must be mounted.

A glorious mass of golden gorse,
A ladybird disdainful,
A kestrel's flight and on barbed wire,
A clump of whispy sheep's wool.

A peer at stamens, pistels too,
Life's mysteries revealing,
All these combined have given me,
This perfect, peaceful feeling.

THE RIVAL

Oh I'm upset what can I do, my man has an obsession,
I think he loves her more than me - at least that's my impression.
I try to keep thoughts to myself, the subject not to mention,
But I must say something quite soon, calmly is my intention.

I've watched her as she displays her fine clothes, her blond, gold tresses,
He always pays her compliments, admires her taste in dresses.
Today I have decided that I must soon have a talk,
You won't believe it even now he's with her on a walk.

I know that she is charming has advantages of youth,
But I confess to share his love is hard to tell the truth,
That he adores and gives her lots of gifts, so much attention,
The fact I'm in the background feeling old, I shouldn't mention.

He's always kind - though it is hard to take a second place,
This is a situation that I'm going to have to face.
When they return their faces flushed with love and happiness,
My rival says, "Look Nanny, Grandad's bought me a new dress.'

Tightly I take her in my arms, her kisses on my cheek,
I love my little granddaughter so much I cannot speak.
I know that all my shopping, my dear husband has forgotten,
But I think now that it could wait to say he spoils her rotten!

LETTER FROM A FRIEND

Though a phone call can be
A surprise and a treat,
There is something I know that is better,
That's the care and the thought,
All the time that is spent,
When you write a heart-felt,
Loving letter.

On the phone I forget
The exact words you've said,
For your voice sounds so strange and so distant;
But the words that you wrote,
I can reread and quote
Everything that you said in an instant.

I can't hold a phone call,
Keep it safe in a drawer,
But your letter with ribbon I'll bind;
You have filled me with cheer,
For you wrote to me dear,
So I thank you,
It really was kind.

THE COLLECTOR

I wonder are you
A collector like me,
Who will fill up a pocket,
With things from the sea?

With shells and with fossils,
Smooth stones, dried seaweed,
If your pockets are heavy,
You're like me indeed.

I walk in the autumn,
The winter and spring,
Curiosity filled,
I collect everything.

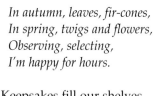

In autumn, leaves, fir-cones,
In spring, twigs and flowers,
Observing, selecting,
I'm happy for hours.

Keepsakes fill our shelves,
And they now overflow,
I must give some away,
That I certainly know.

But as soon as I've done it,
I'm off through the door,
Oh it is so exciting,
There's space for some more!

AIM HIGH

You can do anything that you think you can do,
Just believe that you can then your dreams will come true;
Now make up your mind that a day will be good,
You'll find that you'll spend it the way that you should.

You must now try to change what you think you can change,
To acknowledge, accept what you can't rearrange,
For facing life's problems with calmness is best,
You'll find with surprise that you've passed one more test.

Try convincing yourself when you make your aims high,
You will be a success if you now really try.
Time filled with your love will spread joy as you serve,
Results will be then what your efforts deserve.

If you seek out the purpose in things that you do,
You will find satisfaction is waiting for you.
For nothing's impossible with God as you know,
Believe it and watch creativity grow.

Though sometimes you will find that things never go right,
Hold on fast, full of faith; turn your face to the light.
Frustration will grow if your hopes start to wane,
Think positive; decide that you'll try once again.

It is never too late and you're never too old,
So now pluck up the courage, be strong and be bold,
Don't give up or worry for God is with you,
Then you'll find with surprise that your dreams have come true.

RED IN THE FACE

My friend gave me her washer,
Still good though it was old,
The first time that I used it,
I did just as I was told.

But soon there was a silence,
The still water lying there,
I rang for service, sighing,
Something else must need repair.

I sorted out the washing,
Put it into the machine,
Selected programmes, buttons,
So I'd make it nice and clean.

But didn't I feel silly,
As he grinned and gave a shout,
He'd seen that the wrong buttons
Were pressed in instead of out!

THE LOSS OF PARENTS

When suddenly you lose them both,
Your dear Mum and your Dad,
Your world is suddenly bereft,
You're left alone and sad,
If only you could reverse time,
You'd find the time to say,
The things you wish you'd said to them,
Before they went away.

When tears are spent, still heart-broken,
You feel so lost and cold,
You wonder why there should be pain,
When one has to grow old.
Then God supports you with His love,
And softly calls your name,
He lets you know that they're with Him,
And they are just the same.

Not lonely but together now,
They're happy, full of peace,
And they can start a great new life,
Where joy will never cease.
Your Mum and Dad are close to you,
They know how sad you are,
Where God is, we have heaven on earth,
So they're not very far.

They want to say they'll always stay,
Close by to comfort you,
And when the smile's back on your face,
They'll both be smiling too.
You miss them and you'll shed some tears,
And in your heart feel pain.
But some day you'll look forward to
The day you'll meet again.

THE WEEK BEFORE CHRISTMAS

St. Nicholas looked down on a cold Advent night,
At the villages huddled below,
He smiled at familiar cities he saw,
Country hillsides now sprinkled with snow.

His helpers returned with reports from abroad,
For he knew of the wars and the grief,
His heavy heart lifted for soon man would find,
The right way to bring love and relief.

For everyone working with Nicholas had met,
And in silence had sent out the Light,
They knew God would help man bring aid to the world,
For mankind was aware of its plight.

So love was sent out in the bright, sparkling stars,
To the heads of each country and state,
And comfort and kindness crept into men's hearts,
And good thoughts, for it wasn't too late.

A breath of fresh air swept the world like a broom,
And each house was a beacon of light,
Inside people smiled as stress melted away,
A new hope, a fresh start was in sight.

"They've found us a new home," the old refugee cried,
"I feel better," the sick woman said,
"My son's coming home, I'll not be on my own!"
The tramp smiled at his warm hostel bed.

'Good thought' seeds were sewn, that the wars now must end,
Stopping man fighting their kith and kin,
The starving rejoiced at the food brought to them,
As the Angels sang "God's love will win."

Drug addicts and drunkards found strength to resist,
As God's love and His power swept the land,
The wicked men suddenly stopped evil acts
Feeling sorrow they couldn't understand.

For Christmas was spilling all over the earth,
Filled with love through God's Son's special day,
"If you don't go to sleep Father Christmas won't come?"
Nicholas smile at the things parents say.

St Nicholas sent a message:

"The magic of Christmas is there in your hearts,
And as long as you live you will see,
That if you believe in what it really means,
Then God's love can soon set the world free.

With Jesus' birth, came new life, a new hope,
And with Him you can follow your star,
"Let God be your guide," St. Nicholas cried,
"And find Christmas wherever you are."

A LADY'S BEST FRIEND

She listens to my patter,
And she wants to hear what's new,
She asks how I am feeling,
Will exchange a point of view.

She'll talk about the holidays,
The lottery and weather,
Discussing all the latest news,
Our ups and downs together.

She gives commiserations,
As we talk in a shocked voice,
She sympathises, 'Oohs and Aahs',
And smiles as we rejoice.

She looks at family photographs,
And photos from abroad,
She smiles and shows such interest,
And never appears bored.

She makes sure I have coffee,
Or if not a cup of tea,
And brings my favourite magazine,
And puts it on my knee.

At the same time she's cutting,
Washing, rolling, colouring,
She needs to be quite skilful,
As she answers everything.

She really is a treasure,
Like a priest and his confessor,
I know that now you've guessed it girls,
I'm describing my hairdresser.

TEARING OFF A STRIP

I went to pull the sheet off,
But it refused to tear,
I tried again but strongly glued,
It was tightly stuck there.

I tried again more carefully,
A strip tore in my hand,
Why it was made so badly,
I'll never understand.

I tried then in the middle
To free a single sheet,
But I just ripped some bits out –
I won't declare defeat!

I slide my finger under,
To get this daft task done,
To tear one from the other,
So I have only one.

I think I have succeeded,
Oh no, it's much too thin,
And now I've torn another piece,
This battle I can't win.

Now in a fit of paddy,
I tear a chunk away,
I've wasted lots of paper,
What a way to start my day!

I see the shredded litter,
There lying on the floor,
Knowing next time for toilet rolls,
I'll certainly pay more!

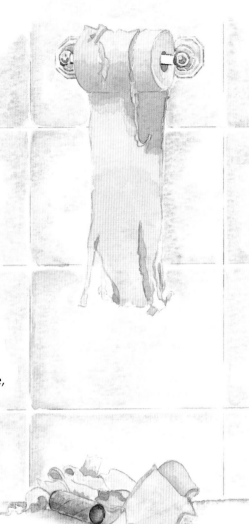

NEVER DESPAIR

If ever you sit down and cry
And wish your life would end,
Just stop and wonder if and why
Your ways you cannot mend.
Because you've reached the low of lows,
Because you're sick at heart,
It's just the moment that God shows
The new life you must start.

It's only when we've felt so bad,
That things can look so good,
It's only when we've felt so sad,
Life restarts as it should.
When summer days are full of heat,
And drought is on the way,
That shower of rain is such a treat,
We're glad the skies are grey.

If ugly things weren't part of life,
How could beauty be found?
Without contrast and challenges,
Dull platitudes would sound.
A runner trains for many hours,
His limbs are tired, they ache,
But for his sport and love of it,
The sacrifice he'll make.

So for that moment of despair,
A hundred you won't know,
A thousand joys are waiting there,
If to the Lord you'll go.
In one small prayer, one word to God,
Faith shown in what you say,
You'll tread the path where hope
  has trod,
For love will pave the way.

God's comfort you will find inside,
His strength will pour on you,
So lovingly forgive yourself,
Free guilt that's hurting too.
Be positive and soon you'll find
Despair has gone at last,
And as you embrace life again,
You'll have gained strength from
  the past.

BUBBLE GUN FUN

We watched with fascination
As they flew up in the air,
So many and so beautiful,
Each shopper stopped to stare.
They brought some cries of rapture
From the children as they popped,
And memories came rushing back,
As we both smiled and stopped.

The rainbow coloured bubbles
Floated high up in the sky,
Way passed the busy, bustling stores,
Bursting as they flew by.
We think we counted eighteen,
Which came soaring from the gun,
A lovely present we both thought,
Give children so much fun.

We bought two but we kept them,
For I thought it would be fair
To let my own two, great big boys,
Blow bubbles in the air.
I'm smiling as I'm watching
As my thoughts are rather naughty,
For the boys who now are using them,
Are seventy and forty!

But I confess I joined them
For I really couldn't wait
To shoot my share of bubbles
As it never is too late
To spend some carefree moments,
With these simple, childish joys,
Yippee, I've now made twenty,
That's much better than my boys!

A TRIP TO BROWNSEA ISLAND

Throbbing engines, rhythmic beat,
Sea-salted air, wind-swept and sweet,
Filling our lungs. Our spirits lifted,
As silent sea-birds dived and drifted,
Skimming our boat in late September.
Oh what a day we all remember.

Proud, stone castle, nestling church
And ancient buildings. How we lurch,
As swiftly we step down the gangway,
So much to see this Autumn Monday,
An Indian Summer this September,
Oh what a day we will remember.

Down the tracks where cars are banned,
Majestic pines, oaks, beeches stand,
Ducks waddle for our crumbs beseeching,
Peacocks lithe limbs are swifter reaching,
Nature beamed in soft September,
Oh what a day we would remember.

Rare red squirrels sat and ate,
Deightful, they were worth the wait;
Sleek Silka deer stood calmly staring,
Seemed not timorous or caring
At our presence in warm September,
Oh what a day we can remember.

Ruins revealed, secrets we search,
We whisper in the ancient church,
Feeding the fowl, the peahens offspring,
We laugh and talk enjoying everything.
A rustic lunch this mild September,
Oh what a day we shall remember.

Time it was to leave behind,
That gentle island, dreaming, kind,
We stepped aboard our senses reeling,
Our island shared our joyful feeling.
We'll come again next year, September,
Then another day we will remember.

MY FISHERMAN

He wanted to go fishing,
He took his rods and bait,
And sat in earnest silence,
From early until late.

He tested many waters,
Around the Dorset coast,
And always came back smiling,
Although he couldn't boast

Of any great successes,
He caught no fish for tea,
But how he spent those hours,
Is still a mystery.

Did he chat to the fishes,
The birds, the bees and such,
His feet get cold and icy,
His back ache very much?

He's really quite soft hearted,
He doesn't like to kill,
I think that is the reason,
My frying pan he won't fill.

You see it is tradition,
My fisherman will say,
"It really was fantastic,
That fish that got away."

FREE CHOICE

Short is the time when you're occupied busy,
Long is the day if you're bored or you're sad,
Peaceful the hours when engrossed in a hobby,
Restless each moment when your thoughts are bad.

Strong are your feelings when charged with emotion,
Weak are your knees when romance comes your way,
Powerful, demanding desires and devotion,
Resistance frail, keeping worries at bay.

High in the clouds are your dreams, expectations,
Low in the doldrums when deep in despair,
Up on a ladder you climb with good motives,
Down you will slide if negativity's there.

Calm is your life now that you've found a balance,
Stormy your life if you don't face your test,
Life's full of lessons, a time to make progress,
You will succeed if you just do your best.

But if like me you find some days a failure,
Nothing goes right or you're struggling with pain,
Accept, hand over to God all your problems,
And you'll find that next day will be alright again.

TACTICS FOR PLASTICS

The meal looked so inviting,
Plaice and chips, oh what a sight,
But when I needed vinegar,
I knew I'd have a fight.

'Tear here,' read the instructions,
So I did just what it said,
I tugged with teeth and fingers till
Frustrated I saw red.

Struggling I tried to cut it,
Then my love said "Give it me,"
He jabbed his fork with great success,
It opened easily.

He has now solved my problem,
So today I'm being bold,
I'll do what he did, then my lunch,
Will still be hot not cold.

Here goes! In jabs my fork now,
Oh how awful! What a mess!
I just cannot believe it,
I've got sauce all over my dress!

WHERE THERE'S LIGHT GOD IS

God's light remains burning wherever you are,
It's there right inside you, a bright, shining star,
It's in your kind neighbours, or loving, dear friend,
It's in conversations when words don't offend,

But comfort and cheer you and never annoy,
Words poured from the heart to absorb and enjoy,
God's light shines in faces, which cheer with a smile,
Which challenge despair and bring hope for a while.

God's light is a welcome, a touch that can heal,
Love filled with compassion, a love you can feel,
If God's light burns low or it burns strong and bright,
In every person the spark's there to light.

For we are His children, we're all made the same,
So ignite God's love, let it burst into flame,
Then pass it around you wherever you go,
When you say goodbye, you'll have passed on your glow.

VISIT TO THE DENTIST

It used to be a nightmare,
I always had such pain,
And after every visit,
I would dread to go again.

I didn't have injections,
And I would jump about,
And all I wished for as a child,
Was my teeth would fall out.

But now it is quite different,
- Although the price is rotten,
And all those dreadful
childhood days,
Are behind and forgotten.

With modern tools and finesse,
I don't feel any pain,
And I don't lose my sleep at night,
When treatment's due again.

My dentist's kind and smiling,
I'm not filled with dismay,
But it is hard to answer ,
With a swab stuck in the way!

Even the sharp injection,
Which used to make me wriggle,
Now doesn't hurt, though
crooked jaws,
Make it so hard to giggle.

But now that I am older,
Some problems have occurred,
My gums are now so sensitive,
Old memories are stirred.

I go to have my check-up
And sit still as I 'oughter'
But shoot up as I feel the pain,
And it was only a squirt of water!

MY SPECIAL TREE

I've a favourite tree, where the boughs hang low,
Where the wind whips blossom free,
Which will weave a carpet of snow beneath,
Beautiful for all to see.

It displays its charms in a gown of white,
Though it's gnarled, diseased and old,
It is loved by birds in their courting flight,
Seeking nectar bees find gold.

When confetti teardrops have all been shed,
For my tree it's not the end,
As the tiny fruits that are tucked away,
Soon with weight the boughs will bend.

Flowers will be replaced by the cheerful grace,
Of its rounded, rosy crop,
What rewarding joy for the daring boy,
Who can pick one from the top.

Then my apple tree still can claim its rest,
It has filled each year with pleasure,
For eternity, it will be for me,
My special tree, my treasure

MY FAVOURITE THINGS

Sunshine and sausage sandwiches,
Smart jackets, perfumed flowers,
Bright moonlight shining on the sea,
And work-free leisure hours.

A meeting filled with harmony,
Laughter and love-filled days,
A toddler's funny, innocence,
A woodland's winding ways.

Pancakes cooked crisp, all sugary,
A loving friend's embrace,
A cosy fire with flickering flames,
A smiling, loving face.

A day free of commitments,
Soft slippers on tired feet,
A cup of tea when I get home,
Is very hard to beat.

A joy-filled dream, a kindness,
Nature, a robin's song,
Recovery from aches and pains,
Good news that nothing's wrong.

Music, which moves and stirs me,
A painting that enthrals,
My time spent writing poetry,
When inspiration calls.

And after I've cooked dinner,
When energy starts to sap,
Those moments on the settee,
My feet on Hubby's lap.

Dewdrops, my meditation,
The first sign of the spring,
Oh I must say I have favourites,
In almost everything.

EILEEN'S RAINBOW

She entered the bedroom and silently crept,
To his side where now peaceful, he finally slept.
Then she held his thin hand and she tried not to cry,
For she knew if he wanted, he'd live and not die.

But he'd made up his mind that it was time to go,
Now his life was all spent and he worried her so,
So he drifted and dozed in a garden of mist,
And he smiled, warm inside as he felt himself kissed.

Then she moved to the window and looked at the sky,
What she saw was a symbol - she let out a cry,
"There's a rainbow my darling, a beautiful sight,
Oh please open your eyes, it means you'll be alright."

How she pleaded and took in her own his dear hand,
But his eyes were shut tight, he wished she'd understand,
He could see his own rainbow that led to new life,
And he tried to convey this good news to his wife.

For somehow they had shared that great symbol of hope,
And whatever now happened he knew she would cope,
He squeezed then her hand for he'd always be there,
God knew what was best, they were both in His care.

THE VALENTINE CARD

When the day came how my young heart would flutter,
Hoping the postman would bring one for me,
I knew my heart would react like soft butter,
If I could but have my own love mystery.

Pacing then racing to search for a letter,
Writing unknown or disguised it could be,
Brown ones for Dad! Oh I should have known better,
For who did I know who would send one to me?

Class-mates, excited all laughing and flurried,
Showed off their cards from mysterious beaux,
Shamed, my head down, pushing past them I hurried,
They called "Did you get one?" As if they didn't know!

They were so modern and my hair was frizzy,
Curly not straight like the belles of the school,
Lifting my desk lid, the sight made me dizzy,
Could it be for me? Oh I must appear cool.

Trembling I opened the longed for epistle,
Blushing as hearts and red roses I saw,
Someone behind gave a secretive whistle,
I turned searching for the unknown to adore.

Many boys mingled with girls they were teasing,
No one was passionately looking at me,
But I could ask —Oh it really was pleasing —
"From whom can this Valentine possibly be?

MAKE UP YOUR MIND

Whatever you decide to do,
In life it's up to you,
You'll succeed if your motives are
The right ones and are true.

Just listen to God's sound advice,
The promptings of your heart,
You'll find that you'll have confidence,
Enough to make a start.

Be positive and persevere,
Have faith you've chosen right,
Encouraged by the still, small voice,
You'll pave the way with light.

So positively see your goal,
Do what you choose to do,
And seeking for perfection's way
Ask God to walk with you.

COMPROMISE

I didn't want to disagree,
So good was my intention,
I only wished to give advice,
And not his friends to mention.

I didn't want to cause upset,
Or seem to be obsessive,
I am his mum and oh I try,
Not to be too possessive.

No matter how I try to see
He is now a teenager,
When he gets hurt and is let down,
He'll come to me I'll wager.

For all I want is to provide,
Security and pleasure,
And though he doesn't think I do,
His happiness I treasure.

If I dislike the influence
Of boys who're wild and freaky,
When I protest and point this out,
His answers soon are cheeky.

"You're out of touch, too old, too staid,
No longer need adventure,"
He thinks he is too big, too sure,
For me his friends to censure.

So I am learning what to do,
'Play it cool ' now is my manner,
I state my case, say what I feel,
But don't 'put in the spanner'.

So now because I am detached,
And don't make heavy weather,
My boy and I both keep our heads,
And get on well together.

THE LIE-IN

I'm going to have a lie-in,
Tomorrow I'll be free,
Instead of getting up at six,
In bed I'll drink my tea.

I think of all the resting
And reading I can do
It'll be a pleasure sleeping,
For an extra hour or two.

I won't set my alarm clock,
This feeling it is grand,
I'm going to bed much later,
As I have eight hours in hand.

Now six o'clock is dawning,
There must be some mistake,
I really cannot stay in bed,
I'm far too wide awake!

REFLECTIONS

What a look she gave me! Oh that frown!
Oh dear she's really let me down.
I thought her always warm and sweet,
Her smile, reactions such a treat.

But now she's almost near to tears.
Her red-stained face reveals her fears,
Her doubts, her weakness, sudden stress,
Completely shock me I confess.

I really thought that she was strong,
Her quick reaction proves me wrong,
I know she's really kind and good,
She's always listened, understood

The need to talk, problems to share,
When she's needed she's always there,
But what she feels shows in her face,
Today it is a real disgrace.

For she looks angry, frustrated too,
I'll wing a prayer, ask what to do.
Ah, that's much better for now I see,
In the mirror, a peaceful, smiling me!

SUNLOVERS OPTIMISM

The first spring sun's the one I love,
It's really such a treat,
It lifts my soul and warms my skin,
And gets me off my feet.

I cannot wait, today is great,
The sky is azure blue,
I rush to get the sunbed out,
I can't believe it's true.

I put the sun cream on my skin,
And find a book to read,
From visitors or appointments,
Today I have been freed.

I've left my work and as there's sport
On T.V. I am certain,
That hubby's really happy as
I see him close the curtain.

Oh wonderful, I revel, stretch,
In golden, glowing sunshine,
And as my eyes were closed of course,
I didn't see the first sign.

The clouds had gathered swift and thick,
Whilst I was lost in heaven,
At ten a.m. the sun was hot,
It vanished by eleven!

As chill winds caught me by surprise,
I felt I could have cried,
I packed up chairs, cushions, sunshade,
And then I went inside.

So I resumed my housework,
Now resigned it was my fate,
But when at twelve the sun returned,
Out I dashed, the lunch could wait!

MEDITATION

Rainbow coloured, light mist glows,
Purple, violet, green and rose.
Slipping softly, stilling thought,
Time dissolves as time is caught.

Reaching, touching, thanks and praise,
Swirling, circling, silver haze.
On the edge of my insight,
Searching, trembling for the Light.

Journey's end is now in view,
God, I'm reaching out to You,
Knocking at your unlocked gate,
Willing now to quietly wait,

For in my rainbow world I know,
You'll show the path that I should go.
Now as you fill me with your light,
I know this day will be alright.

SOUL MATES

Night softened with music as you touched my soul,
Love reached out embracing me making me whole,
My wounds started healing in your words of truth,
As our laughing eyes revelled in renewed youth.

We sang and we smiled as we drank French, red wine,
Our hearts delving deeper now your thoughts were mine,
We discarded food as we couldn't resist
The wonderful music - how I longed to be kissed!

Your arms wrapped around me we whirled and we danced,
Our 'teenage' enjoyment other diners entranced,
As if God had hidden your dear face from me,
Your spirit, my soul-mate was what I could see.

You sang as you held me, love grew as we swayed.
My future, lost freedom, that made me afraid,
Was tossed to the angels in abandoned bliss,
-But oh dearest one, how I longed for your kiss.

That night filled with magic's a memory to hold,
It's worth more than money or rubies or gold,
For Cupid was skilled in directing his dart,
For that was the night, darling, you stole my heart.

WOMAN'S WAY

What pains we women suffer
For our grace and vanity,
Men raise their hands in horror
At our gross insanity.
We take the hair we're given
And we colour it and such,
Then change its style till others
Cannot recognise us much.

We paint the face God gave us,
Which is natural and clean,
And buy expensive make-up,
Beauty soap or cleansing cream;
We take atrocious colours
And we paint our fingernails,
Then exercise and diet
Till we provoke all the males

Not into cries of rapture
But to cries of agony,
At our attempt at glamour,
And our immense vanity.
As we return with auburn hair,
Instead of brunette tones,
"You're not the girl I fell for,"
Our other half soon moans.

The image that we long for,
Oh so willow, gauche and slim,
Reminds him that our roundness
Was what first appealed to him.
The cries of irritation
Which our pangs of hunger give,
Should soon tell us that dieting
Is not the way to live.

A glow of health and fitness,
Full of energy and verve,
Is what we aim and hope for,
We must - if we've the nerve!
For as with creams and rollers
We turn off our loving spouse,
This might be part if what is meant,
When home is just a house.

Let's forget on some occasions,
The thought of what might be,
And be content with what we've got,
And restore reality.

DAD'S TRADITIONAL CHRISTMAS

He loved his Christmas records and he loved his Christmas tree,
Bright decorations, everything that spelt festivity.
He loved his family parties with grand-children gathered round,
When sentimental ballads and dance music would abound.

A table spread with sandwiches, with trifles, salad, cake,
And home made mince-pies, Christmas cake which relatives would bake.
Reluctantly the male members were dressed like Santa Claus,
And mistletoe was hung from lights and garlands on the doors.

Balloons blown up, the Christmas lights were switched on every night,
Praying they'd last till the New Year, we all held our breath tight.
The carol singers at the door, cheeky - and what was worse,
They knocked the door for money after singing just one verse.

The huge turkey that wouldn't fit an oven much too small,
We'd prepared sprouts and stuffing - knowing neighbours soon would call,
Mom's prayers flew from the kitchen that the bird was cooked enough,
That when she served the 'veggies', they weren't cold, the turkey tough.

The flaming Christmas pudding, we were all too full to eat,
Yet cracker pulling, silly jokes we still all found a treat.
And well over his ninety years Dad wanted our admission,
That for the family it still was our greatest, loved tradition!

THE WORLD NEEDS LOVE NOW

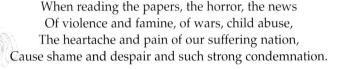

When reading the papers, the horror, the news
Of violence and famine, of wars, child abuse,
The heartache and pain of our suffering nation,
Cause shame and despair and such strong condemnation.

My helplessness turns to the one strength I need,
Where there's only love, help and comfort, no greed,
For I am so certain that our prayers are heard,
That God and mankind by compassion are stirred.

So as we unite in our thoughts and our prayers,
The awakening of conscience affects world affairs,
If only the masses, the world thought as one,
The wickedness, struggling and strife would be gone.

Transference of thought would fly free with swift wings,
And love's intermingling would deal with such things,
That cause such dissention, have rent us apart,
From that power and union soon healing would start.

The rich would share money, the poor would share hope,
The sick would be treated, infirm helped to cope,
There'd be no more wars as man's love paved the way,
With hope in the heart peace would be here to stay.

The drug problem, anger and crimes would be dealt
With firmness and power until God's laws were felt,
It sounds like a dream, a mammoth, hopeless task,
But nothing's impossible if God you will ask.

Then billions of people in every nation,
With prayer, loving actions would protect creation,
As surging of good thoughts save our destiny,
Love would conquer greed, setting the whole world free.

THROUGH THE EYES OF A CHILD

How big are grown-ups and how kind they can be,
They give lots of goodies and sweeties to me,
But then there are times when they take them away,
And say "You have had quite enough for today."

They smile and they laugh at some things it is true,
For others they scold me, so what can I do?
I've heard grown-ups say very often this word,
But when I repeat it their anger is stirred.

"Wherever she's heard it I really don't know?"
Mum didn't hear Dad when he stubbed his big toe!
I wish I knew what makes grown-ups laugh twice.
They tell me I do things which really aren't nice.

Yet sometimes they'll laugh and they find it quite funny,
So I'll try again, oh this honey's all runny,
I'm licking it up from my baby high-chair,
They're shouting at me, oh it just isn't fair!

For they often smile at the things that I do,
Much laughter I get for a moment or two.
But why do they change when I cry for attention?
Their bad-tempered words a small child shouldn't mention.

I'll play with this black stuff which makes the fire flame,
I've done it again; Daddy's yelling my name.
The shouting has stopped now, but I've had enough,
I'll just have a nap. Being a toddler is tough!

THE MAGIC OF MY RAINBOW

I know I can do anything just anything at all,
I am prepared to work hard for I know that I won't fall.
Inside I have the power for God's given it to me,
So if I want it hard enough I will succeed you'll see.

I have all the right motives for I don't want fame or wealth,
I only want to share my love, to be strong, have good health.
My sense of real achievement is when readers words reveal,
The effect of my poems on them, how comforted they feel.

It makes me truly happy if I makes somebody smile,
And every spark of warmth returned makes everything worthwhile.
Some people think I'm crazy taking on this mammoth task,
But my Rainbow is magic so I trust, I needn't ask.

For with such love inside me, my determination, strength,
I'll reach the end of my rainbow with faith not by an length.
My pot of gold is waiting, no, not money I confess,
But when millions can read my words then that will be success!

A FEW EXCERPTS FROM READERS LETTERS

"I have been reading your new book 'Rainbow of Love' and have enjoyed it just as much as the other two books .... I love all your poems but I suppose the spiritual and nature ones are my favourites. As I read them, I can feel my own feelings and sentiments in each and everyone. I find such pleasure in just reaching out for one of your books to read before I turn my light out at bedtime." *Janette Webb, Stroud, Gloucestershire*

"Many thanks for sending the three poetry books so promptly. They are so delightful and already I feel a link with several special ones, expressing a joy or sadness or even how my husband hangs out the washing upside down too! I look forward to collecting all seven of the Rainbow Books and thank God for giving us such a wonderful gift to share with us all." *Wendy Campbell, Margate, Kent*

"Congratulations on the publication of your third book. Yet another captivating book, an emotional roller-coaster of captivating poetry, for every day people of every day experiences. Nice to see you at the BIC last week and looking forward to your next book No. 4." *Josie and Bill Batchelor, Poole, Dorset.*

"Emily is now 15 years old and has been working on a school project which includes you and your poems. ... I read some of her work about you. I thought it was really marvellous. Emily also told me about your website, which I was browsing just now and I thoroughly love it." *Rita Paramore, Almere-Stad, The Netherlands.*

"Enjoyed your new book Chrissy, (especially the 'Hidden Longing' about the nose trimmer,) but my favourite is still 'The Deer-stalker Hat.' We had a good giggle at several of your new ones so it must be good healing therapy." *Joan and John Hurrell, Boscombe, Dorset.*

"I purchased your book, what can I say? I was enchanted, An early bed-time I had intended, turned into a late night, but it was worth it, oh yes it was an absolute treasure of a book." *Enid Halliwell, Broadstone, Dorset.*

"Chrissy how lucky we are to have met you and to bring part of your wonderful gift of such eloquence into our lives. Your books have been greatly appreciated." *Eileen Griffiths, Lymington, Hants*

"Your poems are beautiful and bring the light of Christ into the World." *Christine Benn, Havant, Hants.*

"I thoroughly enjoyed reading 'Rainbow of Love'. It is a splendid balance of spiritual wisdom and pure fun and we congratulate you on your latest achievement and wish you every success." *Brother Joseph. East Herrington, Sunderland.*